HUMAN-CARRYING FLIGHT TECHNOLOGY

Christopher Shipman

BlazeVOX [books]
Buffalo, NY

HUMAN-CARRYING FLIGHT TECHNOLOGY
by Christopher Shipman

Book design by Geoffrey Gatza
Author Photo by Ryan Gibbs
First Edition
ISBN: 978-1-60964-081-1
Library of Congress Control Number: 2011939097

BlazeVOX [books]
76 Inwood Place
Buffalo, NY 14209

Editor@blazevox.org

publisher of weird little books

BlazeVOX [books]

blazevox.org

2   4   6   8   0   9   7   5   3   1

BlazeVOX

ACKNOWLEDEMENTS

I am grateful to the editors of the following publications in which versions of the following poems first appeared or are forthcoming:

Arkansas Review: "Staying Put"
The Cape Rock: "Learning the Alphabet"
Big Muddy: "At the Museum of Natural Science"
Carolina Quarterly: "Hernando's Hideaway"
Chiron Review: "Weather Report"
Cimarron Review: "Since the Toys are Gone"
Exquisite Corpse: "Rivercourse / Last Call"
Fine Line: "The End of the World"
The Haiku Journal: "Picturesque"
La Fovea: "In the grand scheme of things" and "When I was smarter"
New Delta Review: "Fright Night with My Grandmother"
Redactions: "The Last"
Salt Hill: "Fragment from all the Purple Deer" and "Storm at My Grandfather's Grave"
The Offending Adam: "Chop Chop Chop," "Death Writes Home," "The Apocrypha of Forgotten Photos Questionnaire," "The Light in the Dark" and "The Message"
The Pedestal Magazine: "Ruins"
Prick of the Spindle: "Comparing Bones"
Tule Review: "Outside"
Unmoveable Feast: "Snoring through Denial"
Write This: "Just saying sometimes when I'm reading I'm at a bar," "Opening," "Purple Dinosaurs" "The Apartment Pool at Six" and "Young Devil"
"Fragments from All the Purple Deer" was featured on *Verse Daily*
"Rivercourse/Last Call" will be anthologized in *FUCK Poems* (Lavender Ink/2012).

Lines from "Fragments from all the Purple Deer," "The Last" and "Storm at My Grandfather's Grave" appeared in *Metaphysique D' Ephemera*, a play co-written with Sarah K. Jackson that was performed in the Hopkins Black Box theater at Louisiana State University spring 2011.

I would like to thank all the poets, artists, and friends that have supported and helped shape my work over the years. Much love goes out to DeWitt Brinson, Eric Elliott, Benjamin Lowenkron, Brock Guthrie, Kristen Foster, Andrei Codrescu, Ashley Morgan, Jennifer Nunes, Ben Cockfield, Jennifer Tamayo, Susan Kirby-Smith, Leila Warshaw, Jordan Soyka, Mel Coyle, Rodger Kamenetz, and Rick Lott. And for revealing so much to me, thank you Charles Simic.

Very special thanks to Vincent Cellucci, Laura Mullen, and Sarah Kathryn Jackson. Your continuous support has helped me more than you can possibly know. I would also like to thank my editor, Geoffrey Gatza, without whom this book would not be possible. Your wonderful enthusiasm for my work has been a light in my heart. I thank you and Blaze VOX for your courageous dedication to poetry.

TABLE OF CONTENTS

It has become appallingly obvious that our technology has exceeded our humanity.

—Albert Einstein

I, through the terrible novelty of light, stalk on, stalk on.

—William Butler Yeats

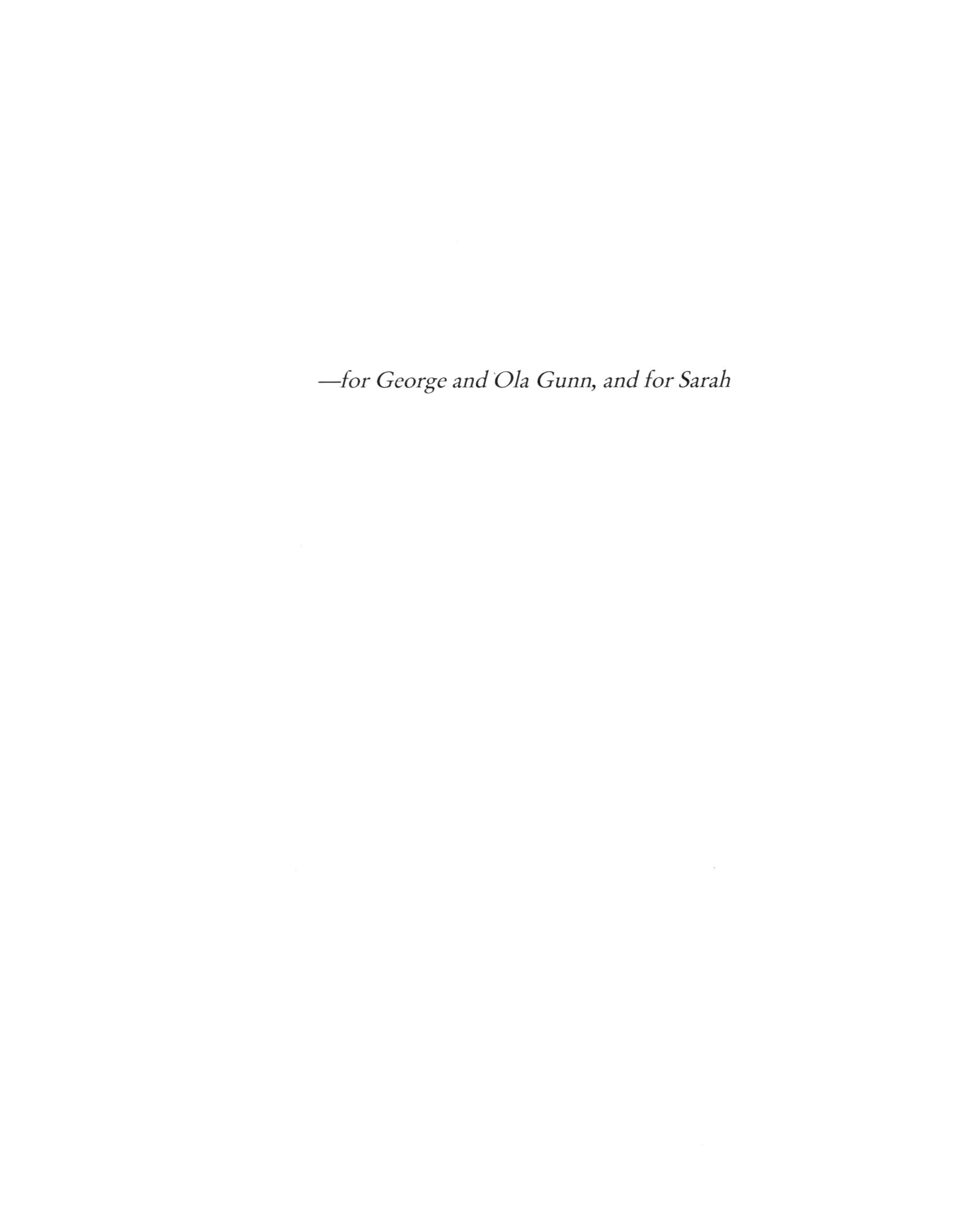

—for George and Ola Gunn, and for Sarah

HUMAN-CARRYING FLIGHT TECHNOLOGY

i   human being theater

At birth

winter came cold as ever.

I curled beside my mother's warm belly,
where I had kicked.

I had taken them all back.

The wind and my mother's voice
hovered above me
when the blue men turned our heat off—

my mother said
            they blued you

with an icy throat.

The summer after
that Memphis winter
half-naked cousins licked candy necklaces—

their necks stained Arkansas sunsets.

I wanted to hold what light hid
in the dark under their warm beds.

My mother said
            I love you

and I leapt from the porch into the sun.

Opening

No one has ever seen inside this orange.

Before being shipped to some produce market
on the borders of Baton Rouge,

before the phrase *Valencia variety
adapted for Florida use* was ever uttered,

before the seedling and the soft soil,
before the mulch and compost,
before the plow, the pump and hose,
before the branches and the sun and the moon,
before the harvest and its hot breath

and blood circulating through beaten earth
kids climbed orange trees and cats climbed orange trees
and so much has happened in the world until now

when picked from a Cabotin's vendor tray
stuffed with brown bags of unsalted popcorn
and ten more oranges, a girl dressed in gypsy rags
for the play she's in, tosses me an orange

across a hallway, where I've waited
for the door to open for twenty minutes.

It's her job to rile up the crowd of parents
who stare at orange programs to find familiar names,
so I jingle loose change, ask her how much.

It's on the house, she says.

I imagine a grove growing from her fingertips.
I imagine my hands are stabbing knives
to carve out the tender flesh.

It's so delicious I want to tear open the girl

when no one is looking. I want
to eat a small segment of her insides, and her fear
of anything whatsoever, while I whisper

little orange lies in her ear.

Last Night's Dream of the Reader

You had a baby that said things like
I bet the movie theater on fire is beautiful to see.

I went in after the evacuation ceased.

Smoke smelled like the bad breath of red curtains
and there was no one to tell any of this to

so we were stranded on a small island.

You had a lover you told a thousand lies to
so we could sail away in the river's reddest wind

with your baby strapped to a turtle shell.

Your lover and I decided to trade licks with an ax.
When I chopped off my own hand instead

your baby slipped back inside your belly.

Rivercourse / Last Call

-for Vincent Cellucci

I

this is as close as you can get
to the river without jumping off a bridge
said the river
said the boat
said the barge and the levee
in its bulging distance
said the kids just across
playing in the yard
said the far away stars in their eyes
said the sex in the marsh
said the bridge and its Christmas
lights when night falls on its head
said hope for
said pray to
said resurrection and o please!
said the dirty sheets on the bed
said like giant catfish said
sweet dreams.

II

the river said I love you
so you leapt off a bridge.

III

the sex in the marsh
the exceptional sex in the marsh
the sex on the levee
the talk about the sex on the levee
the having sex on the levee or in
the marsh
the the
the knee deep in fish eggs
the caviar on the tongue
the pissing it all away
the farther you get
the bar closing
the last call.

The End of the World

—for Benjamin Lowenkron

I

I woke with a mouth full of fish.

My black cat hunched under the sink
by the trash where she likes to hide
when the lamp bulb blows.

Outside, cars stuttered bumper to bumper.
In The Bottoms no one has one that runs
to the end of the river.

II

I'm told by my neighbor, T-Loke,
we were all under water once,
the Mississippi bullied us before
the levee was raised, The Bottoms
what was left when the waves choked back.

III

I woke to the end of the world,

walked to Chevron to buy light bulbs
and a twelve-pack of Miller High-Life.

IV

I woke in a bowl of fish
and the world ended.

Sirens sang careless as sleep.
Sky a coral reef of neon signs.

The girl sleeping beside me still counted

sheep or bottles or fish—
whatever dried up the river in her head.

Everyone was screaming: *we have lost!*

The all-night diner on the corner closed.

No one laughed.

Whole families ran with bags of booze—
their bodies blue behind police lights.

In the distance the sound of crashing waves.

V

The heat is visible here.
Streets clothed in mechanics' rags on fire.

T-Loke told me to watch out for that,
said I might end up a river bed—
cracked and dry.

Sometimes this isn't a game anymore.

I just wanted to sleep.
I fell into a school of fish.

I'm told that's what happens in Baton Rouge—
sardines in a tin can, food for bigger fish,
the Mississippi closed up with us—

the world ends and we're trapped
under its ending.

Hernando's Hideaway

Acquiring the bird was easier
because I was drunk, though that didn't
coax him to come any closer.

Neither of us could sing.
We barely spoke the same language—
the guttural roll of his name.

His *Hernando*-noise rehearsed
fluff— we said nothing to each other.
Though I kept lightly thumping

his stomach, stuffed-animal soft,
until he ran out of cage to back away
and had to steady himself on my finger.

I wasn't scared of the thing
but the fact that it had no song
frightened me. And both of us flightless.

Outside

A pumpkin rots on the handrail.
I smoke the last cigarette before bed.
Night is cold as the smell of old cherries.

Stuffed above the trashcan's muddy rim
white plastic bags dance in the wind
like ghosts of murdered ballerinas
hating the night for falling in love
with so many twinkling toes.

The trunk of an abandoned car
grunts open, its metal the faded gold
of cardboard stars on old movie sets.
The neighbor's black cat rubs an ear
on my pants, leaps over an empty bottle
of scotch, licks my inattentive hand.

Listening long enough to light
wind, I remember my grandfather
whistled ditties, picked cherries
Michigan summers, burned fields
in fall so smoke could raise the dead.

And a grandmother, murdered before
I was born, danced dances I'll never know.

Enough stars constellate that open trunk's
dark smell of used tires, grease, tools—
the memory of a life lived past abandon—
for me to scare off the cat by clapping
my hands, bust the pumpkin I never
cared to carve, and disappear inside
my home, knowing stardust disappears

inside our bones when we're born,
leaving night blacker, and that light
is always flying back there.

The Last

The last flick of the lamp switch
brought her back, an image too in love
with light to blend into darkness without clawing.

The last time I saw her she was reading
in a graveyard, her distance grey as stone,
her thoughts statuesque.

On the way to bed my feet shuffled
against the carpet, collected memory
in crumbs, fallen flakes of egg shell
on the kitchen tile, crisp light

spilling from the fridge, the last drop
of re-bottled faucet water.

In our last fight she threw eggs,
left them to seep yellow
into black grout, the shells
frozen whitecaps on lake-blue tile.

I folded my last page neatly over
a sentence stuck in the dark crease of letters.
The last word I read was *true*.

Tucked under sheets folded over thin light
falling from the window, I heard the stars sing—
everything else you can sleep through.

Fragments from All the Purple Deer

I have loved you for a thousand years
                    is all I have ever said.

Before sleep, hours of purple deer
          prance across clouds like bruised prayers.

Go ahead, blue-black every color of pillow thread
          until I have loved you for a thousand years.

          Morning fog's a sleepy hunter, never clears
this dim city. Birds wake to sing the dead—

before sleep, all the purple deer.

The Apartment Pool at Six

There was another one only rumored by the bad kids
telling half-spun stories of fights,
some boy named Sam or Nick nearly drowned,
or nights black enough to hop the wrought iron fence
and kiss girls smack-dab on the mouth
with eyes closed tight as gates.

The pool by our apartment was way at the back.
Girls slick with lotion had so much tanned skin
I decided the sun must have smelled of peach-perfumed oils.
Summer days I played sailor in shallow water
until tip-toeing along the ledge I felt the depths of boredom
and sunk to the chalky bottom,

where I eventually cut my foot at least ten times
pushing off that rusty drain at the last possible moment.
Once my mother grounded me from the pool
for coming home after dark drenched and dizzy
from swimming all day without eating anything.
I waited at the fence every day for a week straight.

Night came with the first nightmares I remember.
Once asleep I was alone in the pool.
A purple dusk hung above the deep end
where I floated naked, my skin like raked-over dirt,
unready for the shark that busted through the concrete side
and splashed all the water out in one wave.

Because he was lost he couldn't stop trying
to bite my legs off, but they dangled just out of reach
in the drained concave skull of the shallow end.
His dull eyes never wavered until I woke
choking on my pillow, biting a fish printed on its fabric.
I never told my mother about my bad dreams;

I believe boys never tell their mothers much at all.
And I never said how I cut my stomach open
on the pool's pointy fence. It bled out as if ripped apart
by tiny shark teeth, but I'd peeked over at girls
sunbathing in bikinis, their warm bodies close as the sun,
saying something small about the dream of the world.

A Dream a Friend Had Lit by a Cheap Lamp

—for Eric Elliott

A friend of mine
has been looking into the light
for a long time.

How long is the light? I ask him.

He answers by looking
as long as light will let him be.

He never stares straight ahead.

He points to the lamp— *it's there,*
then stares directly at its dull bulb

as if that faint hue has everything

to do with his mother's darkness,
or the blame of his father,

or that it bears the names of both.

Stare at it as long as you can,
he whispers lightly
and looks away.

Staying Put

My parents can't understand
why my grandmother can't understand

their desire to move to Johnson City.
In their own way they try to tell her about the birds

that color the days with their red and blue songs,
that the waterfalls wash away jagged edges of rocks

so there is nothing at all to be frightened of,
that all her great grandchildren, who she watches

dig holes in the yard with plastic shovels
while she sits for hours at the kitchen window,

won't throw stones at her silence,
and in the mountain air of Tennessee

there's enough oxygen for her to breathe
without dragging that rubber hose behind her.

But her husband's bones won't unbury themselves
from their small plot in the backyard of her brain.

They grow new skin everyday— to walk out
to the front porch, to look at things, to whittle wood,

to go inside and make a bologna sandwich, to work
a crossword while she reads a romance novel,

to make believe, to stand on the tip of her tongue
like the tiny god of her thoughts, to cry out,

and to hold her hand while she cries
at his grave just across town.

Reconstructive Surgery

Old women push carts
by my front door
on fresh spring mornings.

The carts
have lawnmower wheels.

The carts
are made of chicken wire.

The carts
are filled with flowers

stolen from the dark earth
under my home.

If I call out to them I drift
like light through
the forests of their faces.

Learning the Alphabet

When the doctor was done
              pressing my face

to the terrible hospital light

        my father handed me the name
hidden in his twenty-year grin,
which must have meant—

        those bones of yours will ache,
        pop, sway, jerk like juke joints
        Saturday nights in July—

then disappeared for six years.

        You better pray, he must have said
when he bent me in half
to hold me to his chest—

        you won't slouch on barstools
        for stiff drinks as those before you.

I want to believe we're not born

with ghosts.   I want to believe

we don't walk over
the un-wearable wings of the dead
spread out on the streets in front of us

like squares of chalk drawn by kids
playing hopscotch.

        I want to believe it
so badly my bones ache.
        I want to believe it
so badly I need a stiff drink

        to forget that the farther I get

from my father the more his image
bellows behind the mirror,

learns to speak
                its own crazed language—

an alphabet of genetics
          streaked in soap scum, that is

          at first a tiny cry, then

a sort of strange aphorism
whispered beneath a scream—

*to name something
is to begin
killing it.*

Love Note

Last year on some dreary Thursday at our favorite bar one of my love's sentences unstrung itself in mid-air— broke apart before it said what it had meant to say. All of my love's other sentences were left stranded— hovering above the cigarette machine wearing Mardi Gras masks, asking the bartender for fruity drinks, ripping off their clothes and frenching on the pool table. The sentence that got away was struck by a punk rocker's sentence spoken two stools down from us— something about the use of sex in punk songs. The sentence had determined to take my love's sentence to the bar's darkest corner, and before anyone could say anything they were gone forever. They hitch-hiked the stars of other conversations, attended lectures on dead languages, spoke little phrases of their own, started an online journal, punctuated mouths of men with long silences— killing braggarts of beauty. My sentences were so jealous and misunderstood they thought it best to keep quiet for good. Every night of their lives this is why I write.

The Trajectory of Curtains

I spend my days trying
to understand

what lights distant sirens
are attached to.

I miss my mother
on the side

like a streetlight looms
over light late at night.

A newly planted tree
can make a kid feel tall

and forget to understand
that when he isn't is

as tall as the sunset.

I'm not doing anything

I often want to stop.

Stop trains
from flattening kids'
pretty pennies:
dream [of course].

Stop busting
pumpkins, etc.

Stop switching lights
off— (meaning?).

Stop writing to walk
by a poetry student
in the nearest future
and laugh, or

not be able to stop.

Last Night's Dream of the Reader

The bank felt more like the DMV
ten minutes till closing on Monday afternoon.

You laughed when I walked in with an old man
who busted open a payphone with his bare hands.

All the change fell to the floor in such a steady jingle
the moon may have exploded at the same time.

A mob of yellow smiles lumbered toward us. I filled
my shirt with change, ran away scared of my life.

I was almost home before I noticed you were gone
then followed a trail of coins back to the bank.

The police had you handcuffed, in line to be loaded
on a bus packed to capacity. You said you loved me.

The worst feeling I have ever had was to know
that you had not at one time, or another.

The Ghosts of Past Protagonists

There once was an old man, for example,
who loved The Beatles.

He told no one, not even his wife.

It was a secret love, like the love a hotel tells
the elevator on the thirteenth floor.

The old man's love for The Beatles was his
second baldness; it was another hat
to hide away in.

You don't know the old man.

If I said he was my grandfather
would you hunt for grey grandfather secrets

of your own? Would you like me more

or less? In this same skin I have now
I waited for him to drive up in his

beat-up truck. I wait on his image to crash
into the house where I waited.
I wait behind imaginary glass with a car radio

clutched against my chest.

Villain on Vacation

I used to love imagining

damaging shifts of what was
understood as A-OK
for neighborhoods I lived in.

An airplane crashed
in my backyard
when I was ten.

A very ordinary power plant
dumped toxic waste
into turtles' mouths
every time I left the house.

Light rain made our ditch
a diseased slick of purple mirrors.

Once the devil held everybody

on my block hostage
for the fall—

a limb of orange leaves.

Tonight the TV's Dracula said
the luckiest man on earth
is the man who finds true love.

I felt for my fiancé's foot
tucked under the covers.

Her red skin flaked away
what the sun burned us with
at the pool all day.

When we got home

I blacked out the sky for her.
I, too, have dark powers.

The neighbors are not afraid.

Picturesque

When I imagine
your skull without skin you are
so easy to love.

Human Being Theater

The blues of your eyes is looking at a light white sparkles of a dress reflects is the winter of nowhere of iced-over ponds we skate into the forests of each other's sad little trees of sequins during carnival season is walking into a piano recital we didn't know was happening until we were gone into the dark is a closed theater is open eyes is a Chinese girl taming a snake if that's the lie you tell your skull to turn your head to hold my hand turn your head smile smile smile!

In the grand scheme of things

a concert hall is full of people

singing in their own marble showers.
          Another full moon empties

                    onto late night pavement

a thousand hipsters smoking cigarettes.

What if they leave and never come back?
If I leave and never come back

I could be going to the grocery store for eggs

on a hung-over Sunday.
I could be hungry.

I could be running around a muddy lake

tomorrow afternoon, or
using an ugly bar bathroom today.

          A lone turd floats in a toilet.

     If I flush it, it will leave
and never come back.

I am so alone I am so in love.

ii   human being curtain

Till You're Good and Ready

My grandfather's red recliner was a throne
in which he cushioned countless coronations
as the tolerant sovereign of our household.
He dozed away most holidays watching westerns
but Christmas break meant movie marathons
he turned off with snores louder than gun shots.
My grandmother smothered him with treats:
tree-shaped gram crackers and peanut fudge
that put him deep in dreams of Michigan winters
he never fully remembered while awake.
At five he had me clad in lumberjack flannel,
pressed Wranglers, and a little boy #5 haircut.
But I kicked around on my hands and knees
like a poor peasant begging for food,
groveling at the snake skin cowboy boots
that dangled off the recliner above my head.
While my grandfather slept his fat Chihuahua
sat like a loyal sentinel. Hidden under the tufts
of a patchwork quilt, he growled at everyone
who walked by with gifts to tuck under the tree.
My grandmother warned me not to get too close
to my grandfather when the dog was knotted
in the quilt- *like a fever dream.* I crawled closer
to the fake Christmas tree, lured by its tinsel hair,
its silver sleeves of garland, its ice-sickle fingers
and pregnant mound of presents, as if it mothered
what my grandfather had dreamt of cold winters
since his first heart attack ripped his chest open.
I grabbed the smallest present with my name
tagged in ribbon and scurried behind the recliner
to sneak a peek at what was coming. The first rip
made my grandfather roar awake, shove his shaky
swollen hand at me and say, *don't you dare
come out from there till you're good and ready.*

School Days

There's nothing nastier
          than the floor of a school bus

where rubber resembles some sticky substance
          alien even to the sickness
of walking back and forth
across a black desert

for a hundred years

as the bus floor's black tar
settles under your shoe soles
more each day

while all you think about
          is sticking your head out
the open window
          into white fluffs of cloud

where you dream
you are your brave friend Jimmy
          jumping off a hill of dirt
                    to soar through a sky

torn open by his BMX bike
for what must've been

          a solid minute

but it's already sixth grade
and your weird friend Ricky says spit
will allow you to live

                    if you're stranded in the desert

Small Stones

I sit sipping rum and vanilla
cream soda.

Do nothing

long enough the birds sing
of wasting their afternoon

notes—

their song of worms, nest, sex,
spit,

the word *sun.*

My dog digs up loose dirt
from our rented front lawn.

If I didn't

demand him to stop
he might eventually find

a former version of myself

still digging to China.
Or worse, a child I once knew

well, and wronged

by telling a tiny lie
about not getting lost.

Then what would I have to say

to this forgotten friend?
I'd have to

tell the truth this time.

Love thy Brother

When I was twelve and he was five
my younger brother trailed me
to the neighborhood park every day.

I felt a strange sort of love for my anger
when I greased the slides slick with butter
because he liked the squeaky zip it made.

For me the slides had slid into everything:
the pig-tailed girl who spun me a fiery look
from the merry-go-round, biting lions'

animal cracker manes into mohawks,
the television set's silver moon before bed,
cartoons, noon rain, swimming in ditches

my mother never knew about, and the soil
softly girdled round a sapling, where I dulled
my Old Timer when carving my name.

My brother smiled when he reached the top,
above the Christmas-heads of young pines,
below tangles of taller trees they pointed to.

Waiting to be lifted to the ladder like an angel,
the devil I saw in him glimmered in his eyes.
I learned to slide into my anger for him.

And he loved me despite what I learned.
One day he seemed to wave from the horizon
hung a hellish red over the top of the big slide.

I pretended not to notice his tiny hand
from the rusty merry-go-round, and didn't
have time to wave back before he fell.

Since the Toys are Gone

Since the toys are gone
we play. We litter
the fresh-cut lawn with wine bottles
and bottle-rockets shot
from the porch with our bare hands.

Since the sign is gone, the crayon-colored
letters ballooning, *PLEASE CLOSE GATE,*
WE HAVE A TWO-YEAR-OLD,
no one cares— sparks fly
off of everything like exploding stars.

The maintenance man must hate us.
But the kid loved it when we busted
the piñata on Cinco de Mayo
and left a mountain of candy,
fake moustaches, and tiny decks
of Uno on his doorstep.

Since the kid is gone his parents don't fight;
the walls don't rattle and curse.

For two years he crawled near the road.
It bloodied all our fenders
when the parking lot finally filled with sirens.

Since the kid is gone
we don't worry if he wanders off.
Since the toys are gone we bless the yard
until our hands are empty.

Callithump

—for Brandon Brawner

Everywhere I see things that care
nothing for me.

A white microwave oven splattered
with spaghetti sauce.

Stacks of books boring as stones
set above a hole.

This threadbare blanket of dinosaurs
roaring to uncover me

from childhood.

I wonder where fears of old friends
have cornered them.

What faces the masks they stack
in the corner.

What roads they march in the dark
distance of hungry dogs

behind their knowledge of being
loved or not.

Human Evolution

The humans crowd around
a white picket fence

in which a standard poodle
punches itself in the gut
with bloody paws.

The humans yell *Abortion is
thinking like a human!*

The humans' big signs read
Stay Animal You Bitch!
in invisible ink.

Story of the Storyteller

The storyteller stroked his dog's ears. The storyteller thought about building a fence. The storyteller noted the nebulous of shadow Sunday afternoon is. The storyteller wrote the word *Vacuous* on a napkin. The storyteller took a drink of scotch. The storyteller saw shadows of oak trees stop spreading over his neighbor's car. The storyteller struck his last match to light his last cigarette. The storyteller wrote the last word of a novel about a city of skeletons of storytellers. The storyteller closed his notebook. The storyteller saw the pile of dead leaves the neighbor had left for his kids. The storyteller had seen them jump in the pile when cartoons couldn't balloon them above the boredom of childhood. The storyteller decided that if they didn't come out to play in the leaves before he finished his cigarette he would flick it in the middle of the pile, where the image of the kid who lay there last burned bright in the storyteller's head. The storyteller said aloud: *if the pile catches fire, if orange flames roar awake, I will stand there crying until my whole body burns.* The storyteller decided that dying by fire would tell the neighborhood kids to tell the story of his name quiet and slow. The storyteller would be the shadow that passes their dreams to say, *stay asleep, stay asleep.* The storyteller tells stories in this way— one decision leading to the next.

The Wrong Floor

Today at the big bank down town
I exited the elevator on the wrong floor.
An old woman with white dreadlocks
had gone in with me and I was distracted.

When the doors opened I followed her
as the white locks trailed behind her
like smoke, then saw that the whole floor
was on fire with cat-shaped flames.

This is when I remembered I had to go
to the vet for my cat's annual check-up
at least three months early because her fur
had turned into a burned down forest.

Walking through the offices' charred ruins
I reflected upon how I had tried so hard
to care for the cat without setting her
on fire, and wondered how I had.

Birds with Long Necks

No smokestacks light this city's dark.
Day lifts into night like a streetlight's
orange buzz. A fistful of wasps nest
sound asleep above my door, huddled like
a hundred shadows of themselves.
The public mood is hidden in the honks
of distant traffic. Last drops of summer rain
are harder than a woman leaving her car
with a bottle of scotch. She checks the lock
twice; her headlights wink. On my deck
I'm thirsty enough for her to turn my tongue
into the oak trunk soaking by her feet, but
I don't say a word when she shakes off
the rain, spins quick as a flash of leaves
in her green scrubs, and stares at me.
A train horn blows; in its absence the rattle
of the broken stove cockeyed in the corner
of my kitchen. The passing train gives
distance a voice that makes me look up.
In the second story of the woman's duplex
apartment, oak limbs shift shadows across
the window and a light switches off.
I look down and the woman has gone
inside. Her door fusses open and slaps shut
in the wind; the streetlight's orange bulb
flickers. I light another cigarette. My neighbor
chases his chickens inside his apartment
with curious caws that startle wasps awake.
Chickens can't look up in rain, he tells me.
Their open mouths swallow so much water
they drown themselves to death.

Impression

There once was a man that was an impressionist painting. The man that was an impressionist painting lived down the street from me and my love. One day the man that was an impressionist painting's belly grew fat with flowers he'd eaten for a late breakfast. The flowers filled his head with wonderment. Was he so anachronistic? Was he truly alone strolling suburban streets in the thick-skulled heat of mid-June? His kind of blue eyes said yes, but his strut swayed no as he dissolved a bit with each step past our apartment.

A summer storm was dying down, and the crepe myrtles were lifting their skirts for the ghost-eyes of old men peeking up through the cracks in the sidewalk, the ones who say, *your mamma's back, break your mamma's back* all day. The man that was an impressionist painting never heard the old men because his lily pads, which my love and I decided were his ears, had fallen off just past our mail box. Maybe he was just distracted by the strange similarity of the pink petals falling from the trees and the ones falling from the bottoms of his soggy pants.

One of the old men under the sidewalk had loved his own mamma so much that he hated the man that was an impressionist painting. And the way he dripped purple paint in the old man's ghost-eyes made the old man slide a dagger through a crack and stab the man that was an impressionist painting in the belly. My love and I watched his guts spill out among the flowers. We couldn't tell where the small intestine ended and all the pink petals began. I got the impression that we'd seen something rather strange, and my love went in to get a camera.

Neighborhood Watch

At dusk the rain lets up.

I step off the usual streets. Search
for the benignity night augustly insists exists.

This is a new neighborhood after all.
We haven't even moved in
a doll's house worth of fears,
hopes and dreams.

There are cars I haven't seen.
Flags in front yards. People on porches
swatting bugs. Flowerbeds dug up
for fall.

At the first turn
from the last familiar streetlight
a black van stops its skulking roll
and talks me out of walking.

An old man, his white hair
a cluster of snow spiders, asks

black dog?

His finger points to where I'd walked
not far from, and his voice
a hand waving where I want
to convince the dark not to seem
so deliberate.

I defer to my own definite *no*, remember
friends who don't live here howling
about how this is such a nice neighborhood—

full of tall trees, good people,
clean streets, the dark lit

by so many pretty stars.

The Apocrypha of Forgotten Photos Questionnaire

In your pretty pictures of childhood joys
where is the memory of a boy burning like a bag of leaves?

Which house hides the kid who slept through winter?

How cold is the image of your grandmother's false teeth
resting among crumbs of bread on the coffee table?

Who is that pulling the lamp's string?

In what locked closet hangs someone's skin?
Whose sleeping face like raked-over dirt?

Why is the birthday girl cowering in the corner,

feeding hunks of cheese to that lost mouse?
How far away are the fields you flew above, high enough

to smile, but not to break when you fell?

What mask is the monster in the dark street selling?
Where is your mother wandering off to?

Eating a bowl of my old wings for breakfast

you may hear the song
I sang to my kitchen floor
one winter morning.

Last Night's Dream of the Reader

My ice-cream was made of meat.

Four scoops piled in a Scooby-Doo bowl
made an old man smiley face.

Your kitchen's bright ceiling fan light
melted the milky chocolate off the top
so I could see the red flesh or rare steaks.

I knew no stomach ache could ever be

as bad as this, so I was thrown
from the roller coaster we rode together

and was forced to be reborn in a ballroom
full of dancers wearing monster masks
who peeked at me through eye holes

as if I was made of meat and ice-cream.

Purple Dinosaurs

*There is a warehouse in California
filled with Barney imposter costumes.*

A friend mentions this haphazardly
on the way to the haunted house
a week before Halloween.

I imagine thousands hung in rows,
on the edges of massive metal hooks—
their purple bulks sway silently
beneath transparent plastic sheets.

I imagine them as one inanimate mass
hung just above a damp, dark floor.

I imagine them as slabs of raw meat
cut from creatures which only exist
in Bizzaro world, which only exists
in the parallel cartoon universe of kids.

Then I imagine the reality of a hunter
of Barney wannabes quietly discerning
the slight imperfections of imposters
in the dusty basement of a Toys R' Us.

And I imagine an imposter putting on
a sweaty purple suit for the last time
before he's finally caught in costume
at a birthday party for a kid who likely
won't remember this rather weird event.

Before I know it we're paying to park
under the overpass. The nearby levee
stands silent as the distance of stars
that carousel above the Mississippi.

Barely visible in the late October dark,
the long necks of bulldozers and cranes
stretch out across the empty river-walk
like purple dinosaurs, searching the water
for what washed away their lost souls.

Entering the haunted house I imagine
the birthday kid wearing a monster mask.
He learns how to make it stay on tight
and how to breathe through the holes.

Necessary Monsters

The butcher's bell rings
when his door swings open
to a small town's main street.

A hooded boy looks out
across a field of fresh snow
from the top of a tall hill
over which blackbirds circle.

Scraps of white wrapper
flutter under slabs of lamb
thawing on the butcher's block.
An old radiator whines.

A starving cat slips inside,
reads last week's newspapers
spread across white tile.
The clock stuck in the past.

The hooded boy hurries in,
hands over a broken blackbird.
All the butcher says is *blood*.

Fright Night with My Grandmother

My grandmother told me to close my eyes
when the vampire guy revealed his victim's tits
to a neighbor from his second-story open window

but then said, *okay, okay open them*
because he was about to bite her neck
and she didn't want me to miss it.

My eyes were closed the whole time
but my grandmother was like this about movies.

She would send me to the kitchen for her smokes
that smelled like old black bananas
or for more coffee or graham crackers
then tell me not to peek around the corner.

She would say, *smother your head in the pillow
until I say to breathe again.*

She always knew what was coming.

When crucial plot points pierced her eyes
as if from a pair of fangs
her voice lunged out and grew wings
and flew over to thump me on the ear.

At nine I must have seen *Fright Night* ten times
though only the parts my grandmother thought
important or boring enough.

I started to believe I was the young neighbor,
who sees what he likes and something he shouldn't
and knows there is nothing in between.

I often caught the mysterious pink circle of a nipple
or the pointed tip of a stake
before it plunged through the heart of a vampire,
but never the burnt skin of the master
or his exploding head
after the curtains were drawn at dawn
and all the glass shattered to pieces.

When it was over I was out of breath,
saw yellow streaks spread
through our small living room like lightning.

My grandmother said I shouldn't
watch movies like that then smiled a smile
that revealed the lightning trapped in her mouth.

When I was older and *Fright Night 2* was out,
which had a werewolf in it,
she didn't bother to tell me to close my eyes
when the vampire guy may or may not
have revealed his victim's tits
to a neighbor because

she didn't like that one as much.

Boomland

Shitting at Reeve's Boomland,
where a bottle-rocket billboard
explodes over the overpass,
marking the largest fireworks store
in Missouri, I have until 1 p.m.
before the bus leaves for Chicago.

A gnat won't stop buzzing my crotch
but all I think about is that
there's not toilet paper enough
to clean the seat and wipe my ass too
so I have to hover above the mess
I make of things, like god.

Seeing *1992* scratched in the stall
I remember we used to stop here
when I was a kid, on our way
to visit family in Michigan.

A huge statue of an Apache Chief
stood guard by the main door.
My grandfather always swore
it was the only exact replica
of my great Uncle Allen, then patted
my head with his sandpaper-hand.

There were fireworks enough
to fill a boy's dreams with dragons;
the light in their eyes set fire to stars,
turned the whole sky to smoke.

I had the desire to play Pac Man
and chew gum for the rest of my life.

I never imagined taking a bus
to see an ex-girlfriend. No halos
hovered above any girl I ever saw,
in any parking lot.

I never swatted at bugs
for fear or their tiny bites,
their mouths full of blood.

That was before I was ever stung
by a bee; before I stopped believing
in vampires; before Pac Man ate
all the ghosts in the world;

before Indians became Native Americans;
before someone lit a match that set fire
to the sparklers; before the Apache
went up in smoke with everything else;

before they rebuilt; before my grandfather
flew to the big hospital in Memphis
and never came back— only bones
in a wooden box we walked past.

A Children's Story

Under murmurs of spring mating songs,

we ate watermelon on the front lawn.
Bluebirds swooped down fluttering wings
for raisins we let soak in the stone bath.

My grandfather fed me pink salted chunks
he'd picked seeds from.

My mother at the creaky screen door

yelled something I'll never remember
even if I sometimes think I do.
There is only the warm lull of afternoon,

shells of cicadas clung to the dying catalpa,
the girl of my childish dreams

playing in the yard across the hot street,

thrusting into my six-year-old lust for skin,
and the love for my mother's voice
buzzing by the acute truth of my age,

which projected just ahead of me
one hundred images of the sun's stillness.

Preparing for the Future

My Darling Love, I am turning into a magic bean. And one day I will turn into a bean stock and then I will turn clouds into a giant and a castle and a dangerous adventure. Will you miss me? I may be too tall for you to hug and kiss me. You will have to climb the stock and hug the tip of the giant's toe instead, or climb his pant leg and flannel shirt to kiss his massive lip. *Nooooo! Why?* I don't know. I guess I thought you might want to hug and kiss a man instead of a stock that used to be a bean that used to be a man. I guess you could just stand at the base of the stock and wrap your arms round and see how far they can go. *Do stalks not have arms?* I don't know. I've never even been a bean!

The Message

A cloud showed up at our front door today.

He was a mess— leftovers of a stormy sky,
all slumped over and trying to pray
in some fluffy language that made us sad,
and it was still drizzling like a failing memory,
so we invited him inside to tell us his problems.

He shook off the grey cold of the grey streets
in our doorway, then ran to the fireplace.

He stood there shivering, his back to us.

When the wind slapped the door shut
he turned to whimper in English,

I cannot remember—

cumulus or stratus— I cannot remember
what kind of cloud I am supposed to be.

We tried to judge by the size of his torso,
the blue tint of his eyes, and what kinds of images
we could make from the shape of him—
maybe a pirate ship, a seagull, a small sperm whale,
something in some way nautical.

He shrugged off our attempt as pointless.

I've been to heaven and back
and all I know now is that I am to find hell
and deliver this message— you are a coward
and I'm going to get you.

Your house just happened to be the first
I saw when I fell.

The cloud thanked us for our hospitality,
and made his way back to the rain.

We thought it strange that god
would entrust a cloud who confuses
fireplaces for pits of hell.

Comparing Bones

The last time we spoke
you were lost in a hospital

bed of wires. I can't remember
your voice, its inflection left

in that cold smell, musty
white walls, the thin light

under the crack of your door.
The ceiling of your grave

is caked with questions–
did I do right by you,

can you rest when I pry open
your eyes, when I fail

to close them? Storm clouds
mimic your beard,

their absence like yours.
Every time I imagine answers

there is never a question. Turn
the earth like fists of a ditch-

digger. Only a glimmer
of your cheap gold wristwatch

would settle your bones.

The Great Confusion

The men made of ears and the men made of leaves are often confused for each other when walking late nights through dark alleys, or when conversing with friends under the bleachers at high school football games, or when waving goodbye to girlfriends in the foggy distance that stretches across train tracks from opened bar windows. When seen from the rainy sidewalks outside those same bars, they lean on lonely stools over something strong and cheap to drink away the fact that it is all going away, that they can hear or feel everything the world whispers of hell when the wind comes blowing in through their jagged shadows from some unseen mouth behind the clouds. And after all this no one can even tell if they are men made of ears or men made of leaves which is absolutely maddening.

The Happy Note

Never mind the sashay of jukebox songs
we can't remember dancing to or not,
last night could never howl louder
than the werewolves behind our eyes.
While we sat sleepless as bar napkins
under all the bras hung from the ceiling
like sideways smiles, I wished they all
belonged to you once upon a time.
Learning to make each other moan
meant leaning into shadows of ourselves
so I said I was a vampire once upon a time,
drank blood from McDonald's cups.
I said I was a cowboy wanted dead or alive,
slung guns Sundays behind the candy store.
I said I saved the world from my front yard
in my favorite Superman shirt faded pink.
The towel pinned around my neck never held
when I flew across the lawn with blue fists
from punching the Catalpa's muscled trunk.
Its dingy green beans dangled above my head
like a thousand nightmares of kryptonite
because you never played with me,
because you went to a different school
in a different city in a different state.
But when I told you everywhere I'd been
you saw Superman scared as Berryman
bare-backed at the top of some big bridge,
and I think you knew I needed someone
the way Clark Kent needs Lois Lane
to know what world he really comes from.
Your werewolf howls fill all my jukeboxes.
You could save my life by knowing this.

Snoring through Denial

How many times do I have to tell you
it is not my snoring, but what I dream
that is keeping you up all night long:
hooves of one hundred snorting horses.

So please don't poke me in the side
and whisper *roll over* when they stomp.

They trample the rough ground beneath us
enough to fill all cold mornings with fog,
to shroud the house where our love lives
with the sound of our long journey there.

So plant a thousand kisses on my eyelids
when they flinch; try to dream horseback.

If you must jump from the flowing mane
of our love, and wake shivering and sick,
even my Irish blood will forget your name:
tread lightly, for you tread on my dreams.

I turn and you've been gone three years.
I've woke to the sound of my own snoring.

A stampede whips and lashes in my ears
like the passing gallop of an apocalypse
I have denied myself to hear— an echo
of a tiny voice in an empty apartment.

Last Night's Dream of the Reader

I tore a few scribbled pages loose
from your My Little Pony journal.
They were burned like old barns
at the edges of wheat fields in fall.

I couldn't save the scared horses,
the thousands galloping in circles,
from the secrets your incomplete
sentences kept hidden from me.

Spring Morning

At 7:15 a.m.

cars lining the driveways
commiserate with condensation.

It's Friday. It's spring.

I love walking a familiar neighborhood
and noticing a rosebush in bloom
I never knew was there.

I close lids of garbage cans in my head.
I send the streetlights love notes
in the middle of the day.

Still there are no birds swooping through
these words. No flowers sprouting
like doodles in the margins.

There are taxes due.

Grandma's dead funeral flower
hung from the ceiling fan.

And concrete.

Noticing Nothing

On the patio at the Milwaukee Art Museum
couples come to look at the lake together.
At these quiet moments they seem truly in love.
They lean on the sun-warmed rail and whisper
about how nice it is that the weather is better
than it has been lately, speak softly of plans
for this evening and the next until their lives
are mapped out at restaurants, with friends
at the beach, climbing mountains, having kids.

A man's hand slides slyly to his girlfriend's ass.
A metal band cranks up a hundred yards away.
A baseball game pushes static through speakers.

This is when I notice the pointed white sails
scattered in the distance, like giant shark teeth
turned away from what water offers our fear,
stupidly try to take a bite out of the sky
because it's bigger and meaner than they are.
Birds better beware such deep desperation.
But all the gulls and ducks lift their heads
to notice none of this, and couples dissipate
like clouds. *I am so alone! I am so in love!*

iii   human being mask

Human-Carrying Flight Technology

If I had my hands on a hot air balloon
its nylon envelope would display
a giant open eye sewn into its gores,

and I'd fly over fields of crowded parks
upon the zephyrs of Sunday afternoons,

but rather than just be thrust along

by strong winds, I'd propel myself though
the ambient air— actuate and inject
a roaring flame into the balloon's open throat

until the crown ring (its hoop of smooth metal)
glistens from the fire to guide my slow ascent,

and because it's Sunday I'd hide myself away

in the wicker basket beneath the shapely swell
of the inverted teardrop above me, and stare up
as fumes fill the vacuous fabric with heat,

to untether the feet of the unhappy masses,
to forget what cannot fly beyond the atmosphere

for all those below who happen to be watching,

who happened to have prayed that morning—
I'd offer them an eye to stare into, an image
of god appearing to stare into them as well—

that is until wind tilts me sideways, and
because I don't know how to fly these things,

the balloon becomes just another bluish circle

of cloudless sky, which closes the eyes
spread across the fields like lowing cattle
(something I also know nothing about),

so I'd switch on the whisper burner, which
I've read is used to not spook cows, then

envision the balloon collapsing after landing.

Springtime Jealousy

The falling honey suckle
I don't mind.

Even when it suckles
my green tea-bag
as if it was a plump tit
exposed in the breeze.

But these bugs
I don't know the name of,
hooked in sex like sex—

ugly antennas—
I don't like them
landing on my hands.

They have sex while flying.
I can't do that.

Alone at the Hilton

I heard someone sneeze
in the room adjoining mine
then both rooms
fell more silent
than a bag of frozen mice.

I thought
for a moment
about saying bless you;
the words half-formed
on my cold lips.

But I decided against it
because I had sneezed earlier
and no one
said anything.

Human Beings and Other Human Beings

Fifteen feet underwater
                         I am
                              still human.

River mud swishes brown squids
                          I step on

                     or wet drawings
                     of squids.

What pretty blood you must have
says the cold current rushing by

                              says
                              my daydreams
bubbling above water.

                     I feel for fish not here.

I am an imagined monster. I am

the drowned victim of a mobster.

I am remembering
                     my dead
                     grandmother

loved double cheeseburgers.

I am imagining myself aware I am
                         human I imagine.

When I come up for air a snake may slither by.

          Someone somewhere is

seeing this.

Someone somewhere else is   shutting off

                     a theater's

last light.

Just saying, sometimes when I'm reading I'm at a bar.

-for Micah Klasky

Let's say I'm in the lobby bar
at the Peabody hotel in Little Rock, AR.

Let's say this is the last stop of a long trip
across the sobering distance of silent rivers.

Let's say I say that only because
I've just read a line about upturned boats
while having a mint julep
with not nearly enough bourbon.

Let's say I need to pee when a woman,
say about 35, slides up to the stool beside me
and asks where the restroom is.

Let's say I receive a long text message
from the friend I'm there to meet.

Let's say he's the new sous chef
at the fancy hotel restaurant,
but his text message says,

let's say, that the restaurant he works at
is actually in the hotel across the street.

Let's say I wonder how I'll validate
the valet, and note the fact that I've forgotten
everything I'd just read for four pages.

Let's say I have no idea where I am
as if I remember every word.

Let's say I'm drowning under an upturned
boat in the middle of the Mississippi
while you're reading this on the glassy banks.

Let's say you say no, that I'm alive and well,
sitting comfortably in a hotel lobby bar,
breathing in the manufactured air
and that I need to pee.

At the Museum of Natural Science

You can tell where a River Cooter's been
by the spirals on his shell— a map of the river
hidden by hieroglyphs only turtles unfurl.
The stuffed specimen at the science museum
stands behind glass, his bathtub claw-feet
pigeoned in by his long journey there.
Maybe he's heard kids kick around on the levee
with gallon jugs of whiskey or wine—
try to be both old and young at the same time
they may have sang though clenched teeth
while the whale songs of barges herded home,
left again, and would one day never return.
Maybe the river has flowed down to him
in palindromes, splashing backward and forward
to say in a word the same thing over and over:
the name Hannah whispered by a love-sick boy
from the flooded banks, his lips redder
than iron deposits in river rocks, his eyes
like turned over kayaks, deep as the distance
between star-clots and clouds. His shell appears
burned by all he touched, all the rotting brush
he smelled in slimy piles, all the nights he spent
alone, all the times he slept through the current
of catfish dreams murky in his head— the lighting
crashes of all he saw— and how it felt to open
his eyes to find the sun hot on the bottom
of the river— the last time he saw spun glass
shimmer on his shell's slick belly, like the last
moment of childhood in a boy's eyes.

Chop Chop Chop

The big oak out back is walking in circles again,
looks more like my grandfather than before—
dead, bearded, fat in the belly, a bulk of grey shadow.
It's always late when this happens, the time of night
when a UFO lands and you're the only one around
to see it. The way it lumbers about is like a UFO, too;
if a tree was a dead grandfather that was a UFO,
it would lumber about in circles like that,
with its head low like a beam of light on a bad street,
the grass swaying beneath as if something alien
hovers above. Tonight he's holding a giant ax
between five leafy hands, and looks especially fat
in the trunk, which makes him especially slow.
It's kind of funny how he tries to chop himself up,
and kind of sad. Chop, chop, chop. One loose limb
falls. He never gives in. I'd holler at the tree to stop
acting like my grandfather as a tree-shaped UFO
but that kind of thing often leads to piles of dead leaves
I have to hunch to clean up the next morning,
the tree standing over me just like my grandfather
used to when we raked the yard, his empty hands
saying the same thing over and over again:
You have to learn how to be a tree to be a man.
I close the curtains and turn on the television,
watch the last half of *Space Odyssey*, every *Hal*
louder than a falling ax. I have learned nothing.

The Guy in the Snow Man Sweater Vest

—for Carl Roberts III

I

Any minute he'll whip out a big gun
and blast my face off.

He glares at me as if I'm not drinking whiskey right,
like he prefers I chew the ice half-melted
in the bottom of my glass.

Maybe he looks angry because he's lost.

He doesn't really belong with the hippies
I see scurry off to nap in the park,
or with the construction workers
who orange exposed gutters with cones.

And he's walked by Molly's open bar window
at least fifteen times— the thirty or so
grey wool snow men stitched across his chest
dancing in the wind.

II

The guy in the snow man sweater vest
bent behind a post-office box
to tie his K-Swiss shoe.

The guy in the snow man sweater vest
lit a cigarette.

The cigarette went out so he cursed the wind
for having a bigger mouth than his
and lit it again.

The guy in the snow man sweater vest smiled
when a homeless man

told a young couple in love
that they were a young couple in love.

Then they all smiled.

The guy in the snow man sweater vest
practiced his strut, just in case a pretty woman
happening by in a fancy dress could get hung up
on a guy in a snow man sweater vest.

He bent to tie his other shoe.

III

I love the guy in the snow man sweater vest
so I have a drink for him,
take an after-sex-drag of my cigarette,
would even do a line if I had one,
off the top of the dirty toilet in the dirty bathroom
with the door that doesn't lock behind me.

The guy in the snow man sweater vest walks
and walks like the people-toed pigeons hopped-up
on coffee and crumbs of beignets.

Earlier, when I realized I was lost
my car was towed and that cost 125 bucks
and it took over an hour to walk to the police station
so then I was really late and really broke and god
I really did want to blast the face off
of the coffee girl who handed me an ice-mocha,
smiling, as if nothing had happened.

And now this guy keeps walking by.
His sweater vest keeps walking by.
And I'm not walking anywhere else
except to piss again, so it's just me and him.

I grab my smokes but leave my book
because no one could love
or hate me enough to steal a book.

I look back toward the table anyway
and there he is baring his teeth to the wind,
waving a hand toward a window across the street
to some unseen friend who isn't me.

Clowns

—for DeWitt Brinson

The clowns live next door.
They make believe.
They watch the clock for fun.

The clowns laugh like harmonicas.
They laugh at our not-clown fights.
They laugh like nothing is wrong.

The clowns smear makeup faces.
Their windows are gross.
They hit the bong.

The clowns yell we yell nothing.
They have parties every weekend.
Their parents are always out of town.

The clowns make faces at us.
Their windows are faces at us.
They mime every time we make faces.

The clowns have mangy dogs.
Their cars are small and judgmental.
They *know you are but what am I?*

The clowns cry every time.
Their make-fun-of-you-faces fiend.
They steal all their groceries.

The clowns turn bathtubs blue.
They soak and soak.
They laugh, and they laugh at you.

.

Harvesting the Moon at Calandro's Supermarket

The small parking lot is empty except for me and a police jeep with its blue lights lit up. National Public Radio tells me tonight is mid-summer night's eve, the hottest June in recorded history.

Summer days the Louisiana sun sets fires to fields by 9:30 a.m., when Baton Rouge citizens are busy balling up suns in small sweaty palms to eat for a late lunch, and I have no desire.

My air-conditioner cranked to full blast and Garrison Keillor reading the Writer's Almanac are all I need to stall my shopping for peaches, black olives, coffee, ink, paper, and soap.

June's full moon was named mead moon for honeydew, the origin of honeymoon, still means a magical harvest for American farmers. A cashier stares. The only magic I can do is feel.

Ruins

The dead should stay quiet.

Night wrinkles your faces again; wind cloudy breaths.
I need to seek my own madness: sun-lit hours, fists,
shattered glass. But ancient wolfhounds wait

by my front door, lick foggy chops, scratch muddy paws across
my welcome mat. Let their mouths sleep. Tell one secret

a day until all their bleeding teeth rot. Offer them
blueberries before they sour, fallen apples yet unfolded,
softly browned in unturned orchards.

Great grandfather, you died alone—

farmer of war, six kids, ships where you stowed memory.
I can't close your eyes from store windows. You see through dirt.
And you, his wife, hunched in bed. How did it come to this—

your tongue clung to ice chips, gasping on cotton swabs?
Every time I watch you die, I am born into this. Your last

whimpers can still end the world. I see your secrets
float out again, slink into the lonesome must of living,
crowd against the white ceilings of white hospital rooms—

a gathering of ghosts, ruining light.

Death Writes Home

Dear mother, I have found a home
in the world and won't be returning
to the darkness save holidays.

Tell Life she can have my room.
She always wanted it anyway.
She loves the bay window
that shows the big oak out back.

Father had promised to carve
a clubhouse into it with his big toe
it must be a thousand years ago.
Is he still making Life call him God?
God this God that goddamn it all!

Well, make sure she walks the dog
but that she keeps off Lucifer's lawn.
You know how he hates dog shit
and gets all red and hot in the face
whenever he eyes that little mutt.

Resurrection says hi. She grew a heart
and breasts for me! We got hitched!
It was a bit strange being in Vegas
without tugging a dead hooker
out of some locked-up icebox.

I'm sure father mentioned it.
We wrote our own wedding vows
and I know how he hates that.
I wonder what he thought of me
dressed as a sequined velvet Elvis.

Well, that's what I'm about now.
May be a good idea to have a baby
or start digging up skeletons, I guess,
to find a good place to put my past.

Growing a tongue felt like dying,
by the way, but when I lean in to kiss
my beautiful bride she's full of light.

Discussion of the Earth-bound Angels

Charles (sighs):

I have found that I only like stories
about the carelessness of hikers
trapped at the tops of mountains

but even then
only when I have heard so much song
float from the black branches of morning
that not even birds listen in.

Bob (frowns):

What do you mean?

Charles (stands upside-down):

What do you mean by what do you mean?
This is what I have found!

Mountain (fears god):

The heaven hidden above them
applauds loud and unclear.

I feel I must

say now
how I adore
life's little
affectations
when your
aqua nail polish
lit by dim
bar lights
appears
chipped
at the ends
like angels
pretending
to be birds.

Roller Rink on Fire

The man who reads the traffic report
for the university radio station
sounds much older than all the DJ's,
doesn't say things like, *like*
after every short phrase.

Driving anywhere during rush hour
usually means his strange way of saying—
we have some accidents working.

And his voice aged another ten years today,
when instead of detailing the eagle eye view
of the scene from the company helicopter
like a traffic jam of matchbox cars lined up
at a kid's fingertips, he said—

the old roller rink on North Street
          is burning.

He paused at the end of his sentence,
unsure of the unsteady beat of his own breath,
as if his memory of the place burned with it.

I turned the station to static, wondered why
images mean so much to us
while white puffs of smoke rolled
from the old roller rink back home,
a solid day's drive away,
where my mother is still inside
lacing up my skates.

Black streaks smudge across the floor.
The strange squeak of wheels scares me
enough for my mother to smile again.

Behind the grey wall I rest my back against
thick traffic circles rolling flames.

Same As It Ever Was

Church bells ring in the distance.

A mailman moves his earmuffs
to hear the same nameless song as ever.

His boots push through piled leaves,

which content on the insistent sidewalk
long ago forgot the feeling of falling.

He slides a letter through the slot

of a home quieted by winter,
and its abandoned garden of stiff roots.

Inside, a slack-jawed dog watches

a housewife fry strips of turkey bacon.
The purple stain splotched on the stove

a week older than the last sip of wine.

The widowed neighbor's lotto number
wins big, so she praises her god's

relative distance. No one hears this.

A waiter waits on the Sunday crowd to pour through the doors. He considers well-postured demons in church pews wishing to wash out their mouths, rid the duende whispering their names asunder, while the true believers doze into dreams of pizza. Which is he is what he doesn't wonder.

The Religion of Pizza

The god in me sulks
like the alley behind Pizza Hut
when I was eleven.

Boys smoked back there.
Boys hid from parents.
Boys grew werewolf hair.

The god in me didn't even score
against the Whirlwinds
or the Hurricanes or the Cyclones.

The god in me only beat
Green County Tech,
who had a quarterback shorter
than the blockers protecting him.

But my father coached me
on buffets anyway: *eat
all you can,* he said.

The god in me eats.

The god in me sleeps
beside the first girl I slept with
who slept beside an old pizza box
in the back seat
of my mother's pink Pontiac.

The god in me wakes
to write his name in all caps
on the fogged-up back glass
then falls again like the devil
into dreams of lowercase
glossolalia.

I wish the god in me
would grow up, stop whining
about whatever hell he's in
and take me out for beer and pizza.

Young Devil

Jeremy used to burn his sister's Barbie dolls
on his mother's rusty yellow stove.

He'd sit them two at a time
in semi-sexual positions
on the big back burner,
and silently watch
as hairspray and lighter
made a blue and orange torch.

Their fancy dresses unfolded in the flames first.
Then the soft blond hair caught fire,
shriveled up in one smelly singe.

But when the plastic skin started to bubble,
and the tiny breasts popped
like two short-fused fireworks
the smell was unbearable.

And the god-awful sight of the whole mess
dripping beneath the burner's rusty rings
was enough for me to excuse myself.

Time for lunch I'd tell him,
not knowing then that my remark
could have been the funny punch-line
to the whole devilish event.

Once home I'd make He-Man
make slow, sweet love to She-Ra,
mostly kissing and grinding at awkward angles.

Weather Report

Sleet in some parts of the city—
said the static of local radio news
as the first icy flakes fell
and cracked quietly against my car.

On the drive to school
you hoped campus had closed
like a child leaning coldly over
a bowl of morning cereal.

When I dropped you off
you kissed me twice
and took my broken
black umbrella to blend you in
with the dark noon sky's
out of tune piano.

Home alone with Beethoven
concertos, I pick apart pipe tobacco
and sip hot coffee to stay awake.

I am nothing like a child.

When sleet stops tipping its hat
the sky's silent anthem
is a plaintive fade into sunshine.

I heat up Italian leftovers
and work all day— all the while
I miss you like I miss being a child.

Jaw

It is difficult
to get the news from poems
*   yet men die miserably every day*
*   for lack*
of what is found there.

     —William Carlos Williams

When a semi-tropical town
in southern Louisiana talks
of possible ice accumulation
(even less than half an inch)
and streets listen in late at night—

when some drunk falls
among silent streetlights
outside a lover's dark house
then yells out to no one: *ice*
has been here all along—

when the cold morning clerks
at the gas station near the airport
hear planes halt, when schools
close, when children slip back
to bed, when food sales boom—

the steady ache of language,
its dream of the open mouth
is a frenzy of delirious dogs
fighting over a raw steak
wrapped in newspaper.

At winter's end

a second line waits
with trumpets at the airport
to sing souls' last names.

Last Night's Dream of the Reader

I

In the city of every city I've ever been
a thousand clouds shift shapes across a sun

I wouldn't dream of deciphering.

I sit still as a star in a small trolley
sliding down the hill of a worn sidewalk.

You are a beautiful woman with short hair
the color of hay wet with rain.

You are about to jog off into the woods.

When the trolley stops I let you get
a good thirty second head start.

The heart tied to your ankle drags behind you,

beats down weeds, packs dirt into a path.
I wait till you turn to see me waiting.

I drop to all fours and gallop after you.
In my mouth a monster is mean with hunger.

You smile when I tear off your leg.

II

Outside your house we are shrouded in pines
when you tell me your friends have arrived.

Each one has a name, a face, a fashion sense.

They're so happy it's not long before they've gone
into the blank white space between my eyes

and the you of my dreams squatting on a log.

We exchange faces, walk through the woods
without moving the mouth of the other.

You come to a house where my memory lives.

Hidden within dark cherry wood walls
you pry loose the script of my existence—

images of birth, death, all the ugly birds

I am ashamed of, my hunching in the corner,
my staring at you, my staring at you, etc.

III

I buy a small dog just to walk by your house
on the way to the neighborhood veterinarian.

Your leaves are so pretty you don't see me.
When you leave the view of your open window

I climb your ivied lattice and sit on your bed.

You stroll over to kiss my miracle of arrival.
Your lips taste like the cherries of my past.

I offer to buy new beautiful furniture for you.
I wake with a terrible taste in my mouth, a black

hole.

The Light in the Dark

One Sunday we woke to what we thought to be early morning, pre-dawn darkness, and the screeching sounds of the neighborhood hawk poking its bloody beak into some smaller half-dead bird. So, we went back to our pillowcases with American dreams of brunch at the bistro.

After three hours our late-sleeper bones shook us awake. When we opened the blinds whole families were walking down the street out front, looking up. My cell phone said noon but the day was black as an imagined dark at the end of a tragic novel. And there were no birds at all— just children rubbing sleep from their eyes, blinded by the absence of birds.

It was on every channel. The news showed clips of New York City, London, Dubai, etc. The only light in the dark was riot fires in front of every cameraman. The sun was simply gone.

A few days ago the fires finally died down. Now all the blind children run around naked, bats nest in the grocery stores, shriveling houseplants hide in the corner. No one knows when it's going to rain, or when to have a lazy day, or what kind of music to listen to, what to do with the family of wolves on the back steps, with shadows, with all the sweaty dreams of sunlight.

It's Sunday again. This morning we woke to what we thought to be the puppy whimpering beside the bed, needing to pee. I reached to grab him and burned my hand on something. Fearing a fire I hunched by the bed to see a tiny sun cowering in the corner of the baseboards, like some lost orphan, burning black rings in the floor as he tried to roll away.

We've discussed keeping him as our own son. I'm not sure how to raise him, feed him, or teach him. What kind of clothes does the sun wear? I don't know why he chose us, but I'm so happy I don't think about all those blind kids out there.

Storm at My Grandfather's Grave

Rain must be made of bones,
each drop dust, someone's once more
denied attempt to soar from this world.

Where do you wish to fly? To what star?
I ask you because you have gone.

I ask you because you have fallen
more times than I have stood.

Water stands in my boots.
All is a misunderstood prayer.

If there's a point, a meeting between
the light and dark, it's joined as a palm
collecting rain.

On the way home

I told
a waitress
at Waffle House
about the overturned
car I saw
ablaze on the freeway
all fire and wheels.

He was going
north I said
but I was going
south I said.

I wonder
now
why I said that.

When I was smarter

I once drew a dead zebra on a bathroom stall.

I wonder if anyone ever wishes
there is a number to call.

The noose around the neck

                likely dangles a deterrent.

Mosquitos bite
late parking lot nights
anyway it goes.

Hundreds and hundreds of kids continue
                to check yes or no for love.

So much seems so much

easier than bathroom stalls
                offering blowjobs.

So much seems so much better
than blood,

but truck stops will never be

                as sleazy as imagination.

The sun doesn't shake his head
at my sexist pronoun

or for anything else.

Men's Restroom 3rd Stall Meet Me There

Every time it's just me in a public restroom
I think everyone who walks in
wants to chop down the door of my stall
with a bloody ax.

Someone strolls in
and I choke up a cough,
sniff a bit as if I'm about to sneeze
into the moth-dingy light above me,
let out the demons my mother always said
she blessed me for.

The murderers I imagine
wouldn't dream of killing me
in the fits of a cold.

I invite no one into my maybes.
I own all the axes in the world.

The guy beside me wears Air Jordan's.
All I can see are 23's
and a pubic hair stranded under his right shoe.
I wait to leave until he does.

I am so alone! I am so in love!

Christopher Shipman lives in Baton Rouge, LA with his wife Sarah, his dog George, and his two cats, Jack and Adele. He received a MFA in poetry from Louisiana State University in 2009. His poems have appeared in literary journals such as *Cimarron Review, Exquisite Corpse, The Offending Adam, Pedestal,* and *Salt Hill,* among many others. Shipman is poetry editor for *DIG Magazine* of Baton Rouge and teaches at Baton Rouge Community College.

Made in the USA
Monee, IL
07 July 2026